AI Disclaimer

The content of this book is generated with the assistance of artificial intelligence (AI) technology. While every effort has been made to ensure the accuracy and reliability of the information presented, the author and publisher acknowledge that AI-generated content may not always reflect the most current research, expert opinions, or best practices in the field. Readers are encouraged to use their own judgment and consult relevant sources or professionals when applying the concepts discussed in this book. The author and publisher disclaim any liability for any errors, omissions, or consequences arising from the use of this material. This book is intended for informational purposes only and should not be considered a substitute for professional advice. By engaging with this content, you acknowledge and accept this disclaimer.

Table Of Contents

Chapter 2: The Pros and Cons of Understanding Blockchain 2

Chapter 3: Financial Services: Impact of Blockchain on Banking and Investment Strategies 2

Chapter 4: Supply Chain Management: Benefits and Challenges of Transparency in Logistics 2

Chapter 5: Healthcare: Implications of Blockchain for Patient Data Security and Interoperability 2

Chapter 6: Real Estate: How Blockchain Affects Property Transactions and Ownership Verification 2

Chapter 7: Education: The Role of Blockchain in Credential Verification and Academic Records 2

Chapter 8: Government: Pros and Cons of Using Blockchain for Public Records and Voting Systems 2

Chapter 9: Cybersecurity: Understanding Blockchain's Security Features Versus Potential Vulnerabilities 2

Chapter 10: Energy Sector: The Influence of Blockchain on Renewable Energy Trading and Distribution 2

Chapter 11: Digital Identity: The Advantages and Risks of Blockchain-Based Identity Solutions 2

Chapter 12: Entertainment and Media: Effects of Blockchain on Copyright Management and Content Distribution 2

Chapter 13: Conclusion: The Future of Blockchain for Investors in 2025 2

Chapter 1: Introduction to Blockchain in 2025 3

Chapter 1: Introduction to Blockchain in 2025

Overview of Blockchain Technology

Blockchain technology is a decentralized digital ledger system that records transactions across multiple computers in such a way that the registered transactions cannot be altered retroactively. This innovative approach ensures transparency, security, and trust among participants, as every transaction is time-stamped and linked to the previous one, creating an immutable chain. The core principles of blockchain—decentralization, transparency, and security—are revolutionizing various sectors by providing a new way to manage and verify transactions without relying on a central authority. As we navigate the blockchain landscape in 2025, understanding these foundational concepts becomes crucial for investors and stakeholders across industries.

In the financial services sector, blockchain is reshaping banking and investment strategies by enhancing efficiency and reducing costs. Traditional banking systems often rely on intermediaries for transactions, which can introduce delays and increase fees. By implementing blockchain, financial institutions can streamline processes, allowing for near-instantaneous transfers and settlements. Additionally, smart contracts—self-executing contracts with the terms of the agreement directly written into code—enable automated and trustless transactions, thereby minimizing the need for third-party oversight. However, this disruption also raises concerns regarding regulatory compliance and the potential for market volatility as established financial systems adapt to this new technology.

Supply chain management stands to benefit significantly from blockchain's inherent transparency and traceability. By incorporating blockchain into logistics, companies can provide real-time tracking of goods, ensuring that all parties have access to the same information. This transparency helps to reduce fraud, improve accountability, and enhance the overall efficiency of supply chains. Nevertheless, the implementation of blockchain in this area is not without challenges. Issues such as the integration with existing systems, data privacy concerns, and the need for industry-wide cooperation can complicate the rollout of blockchain solutions in supply chain management.

In healthcare, blockchain holds promise for enhancing patient data security and interoperability. By allowing patients to control access to their medical records through a secure blockchain system, healthcare providers can ensure that sensitive information is shared only with authorized individuals. This approach can improve patient outcomes and streamline care coordination. However, the adoption of blockchain in healthcare also poses challenges, such as the need for standardization and the potential for data breaches if security measures are not adequately implemented. Thus, while the implications of blockchain are significant, they require careful consideration and planning.

The impact of blockchain extends to various other sectors, such as real estate, education, government, cybersecurity, energy, digital identity, and entertainment. In real estate, blockchain can simplify property transactions and enhance ownership verification, reducing fraud and streamlining processes. In education, it offers a reliable method for credential verification, ensuring the integrity of academic records. Government applications of blockchain can improve public records management and voting systems, although concerns about privacy and security need to be addressed. In cybersecurity, blockchain's security features provide robust protection against data tampering, yet vulnerabilities remain that must be understood. Similarly, the energy sector can leverage blockchain for efficient renewable energy trading, while digital identity systems based on blockchain can enhance privacy and reduce identity theft risks. The entertainment industry benefits from improved copyright management and content distribution, though challenges in implementation persist. As these diverse applications evolve, understanding the pros and cons of blockchain technology in 2025 becomes essential for all stakeholders involved.

The Evolution of Blockchain: Past, Present, and Future

The evolution of blockchain technology has been a profound journey, beginning with its inception in 2008 through the publication of Satoshi Nakamoto's white paper. The concept of a decentralized digital currency emerged as a response to the global financial crisis, highlighting the need for a system that operates independently of central authorities. The initial focus was primarily on Bitcoin, which introduced the idea of a secure, immutable ledger that could facilitate peer-to-peer transactions. Over the years, the technology underlying Bitcoin was recognized for its broader applications, leading to the development of various other cryptocurrencies and projects that sought to harness blockchain's potential in diverse fields.

In the present day, blockchain has transitioned from a niche technology to a mainstream solution with applications spanning various industries. Financial services have seen a significant impact, as banks and investment firms explore blockchain to enhance transaction efficiency, reduce costs, and improve security. Smart contracts, which automatically execute agreements when conditions are met, have further transformed investment strategies, enabling more secure and transparent deals. The integration of blockchain into supply chain management has also gained momentum, providing unprecedented transparency and traceability, which are crucial for combating fraud and improving logistics efficiency.

Looking ahead to 2025, the future of blockchain holds immense promise, but it is not without challenges. In healthcare, for example, blockchain offers potential solutions for securing patient data and achieving interoperability between different healthcare systems. However, issues such as regulatory compliance and integration with existing infrastructures must be addressed to realize these benefits fully. Similarly, in real estate, blockchain can streamline property transactions and enhance ownership verification, yet the adaptation of traditional practices to this new technology poses obstacles that must be navigated carefully.

In the realm of education, blockchain's role in credential verification is gaining traction, allowing institutions to issue tamper-proof academic records. This development can enhance trust in educational qualifications, but it also raises questions about privacy and data ownership. Governments are exploring the use of blockchain for public records and voting systems, presenting both opportunities for increased transparency and concerns regarding accessibility and security. As various sectors evaluate the pros and cons of blockchain, it is clear that stakeholder engagement and collaboration will be essential.

As blockchain technology continues to evolve, its implications for cybersecurity, digital identity, and even the energy sector are becoming increasingly relevant. By offering enhanced security features and decentralized identity solutions, blockchain can mitigate risks associated with data breaches and identity theft. In the energy sector, it is poised to revolutionize renewable energy trading and distribution, fostering a more decentralized and efficient energy market. As investors and stakeholders navigate the blockchain landscape in 2025, understanding the historical context, current trends, and future potential of this technology will be critical to making informed decisions in an ever-changing environment.

Importance of Understanding Blockchain for Investors

Understanding blockchain technology is crucial for investors in 2025 due to its transformative potential across multiple sectors. As financial services increasingly adopt blockchain for transactions and record-keeping, investors must grasp its implications on banking and investment strategies. The decentralized nature of blockchain can reduce costs, enhance transaction speed, and improve transparency, fundamentally altering how financial institutions operate. Investors equipped with this knowledge can make informed decisions that align with the evolving landscape of financial technology, ensuring they capitalize on new opportunities while mitigating risks associated with traditional systems.

Supply chain management is another area significantly impacted by blockchain. The technology offers unprecedented levels of transparency and traceability, enabling companies to track products from origin to consumer. For investors, understanding how blockchain enhances logistics can inform investment in companies that adopt these practices, potentially leading to greater operational efficiencies and reduced fraud. However, challenges such as integration costs and the need for industry-wide standards must also be considered. Investors who comprehend both the benefits and hurdles will be better positioned to evaluate the long-term viability of blockchain initiatives in supply chains.

In healthcare, blockchain's implications for patient data security and interoperability make it an essential area for investors to understand. As the healthcare sector grapples with data breaches and fragmented records, blockchain promises a unified system where patient information is securely stored and easily accessible across platforms. This advancement not only enhances patient care but also presents investment opportunities in companies pioneering blockchain solutions for healthcare. However, investors must also be aware of regulatory considerations and the potential for industry resistance, as healthcare institutions may be slow to adopt new technologies.

The real estate market is undergoing a transformation driven by blockchain technology, particularly in property transactions and ownership verification. The ability to create immutable records of property ownership can streamline transactions and reduce fraud, making blockchain an attractive proposition for investors in this sector. Understanding the legal implications and potential disruptions caused by blockchain in real estate will allow investors to identify profitable ventures while navigating potential challenges, such as regulatory hurdles and the need for widespread industry acceptance.

Finally, blockchain's role in digital identity and its application in various sectors, including education and government, presents a dual-edged sword for investors. While blockchain-based identity solutions can enhance security and reduce identity theft, they also raise concerns about privacy and data misuse. Moreover, in education, the technology's potential for credential verification can revolutionize hiring processes, while in government, its use for public records and voting systems can enhance transparency but may face public skepticism. Investors who grasp these nuances will be better equipped to discern the viability of blockchain applications across different industries, enabling them to make strategic, informed investments in an increasingly blockchain-driven world.

Chapter 2: The Pros and Cons of Understanding Blockchain

Benefits of Blockchain Knowledge for Investors

Understanding blockchain technology offers a multitude of benefits for investors across various sectors. As blockchain continues to evolve, investors who grasp its fundamental principles can make informed decisions that significantly impact their financial strategies. Knowledge of blockchain equips investors with the ability to identify opportunities in emerging markets, assess risks more effectively, and adapt to the rapid technological changes that characterize the investment landscape of 2025. Recognizing the potential applications of blockchain can lead to advantageous positions in sectors such as financial services, supply chain management, healthcare, and beyond.

In the financial services sector, blockchain technology is revolutionizing banking and investment strategies. Investors with blockchain knowledge can leverage decentralized finance (DeFi) platforms, which provide new avenues for lending, trading, and asset management. This understanding enables investors to navigate the complexities of digital currencies and tokenized assets while enhancing their portfolio diversification. Additionally, awareness of blockchain's impact on transaction speed and cost can lead to more strategic investment decisions, allowing investors to take advantage of lower fees and faster settlement times.

Supply chain management also benefits from blockchain transparency, which investors should comprehend to evaluate logistics investments. Knowledge of how blockchain enhances traceability and accountability throughout the supply chain can inform decisions about investing in companies that prioritize sustainable and ethical practices. Investors who understand the challenges and benefits of implementing blockchain in logistics are better positioned to assess the long-term viability of their investments in this area, especially as consumer demand for transparency grows.

In healthcare, blockchain's implications for patient data security and interoperability present unique investment opportunities. Investors who grasp how blockchain can safeguard sensitive health information while facilitating seamless data sharing between providers can identify promising healthcare technology firms. This knowledge not only aids in evaluating the security measures of potential investments but also highlights the growing demand for innovative solutions that enhance patient care and operational efficiency within the healthcare system.

Finally, as blockchain technology increasingly influences sectors like real estate, education, government, and energy, investors must understand its implications for property transactions, credential verification, public records, and renewable energy trading. Each of these areas presents distinct investment opportunities, alongside potential risks that can be mitigated through informed decision-making. By staying informed about the evolving landscape of blockchain, investors can strategically position themselves to capitalize on the benefits while navigating the complexities and challenges that come with these technological advancements.

Risks Associated with Ignorance in Blockchain

Ignorance regarding blockchain technology presents significant risks across various sectors, particularly for investors, corporations, and educational institutions. In the financial services sector, a lack of understanding can lead to poor investment decisions. As blockchain disrupts traditional banking and investment strategies, those not versed in its implications may miss opportunities or engage in transactions that expose them to unforeseen risks. The volatility associated with cryptocurrencies and blockchain-based assets can be exacerbated by ignorance, making it crucial for investors to grasp the fundamental principles of this technology to navigate the landscape effectively.

In supply chain management, ignorance of blockchain's capabilities can result in inefficiencies and vulnerabilities. The technology offers enhanced transparency and traceability, which are essential for logistics and inventory management. However, companies that fail to understand how to implement blockchain solutions may struggle with outdated practices, leading to increased costs, delayed shipments, and compromised product integrity. Furthermore, without a clear understanding of the technology, organizations may overlook potential partnerships or innovations that could enhance their supply chain processes.

The healthcare industry faces unique challenges associated with ignorance of blockchain's potential for patient data security and interoperability. With data breaches becoming increasingly common, blockchain offers a solution for securing sensitive patient information while ensuring seamless access across different health systems. However, stakeholders who do not comprehend how to leverage blockchain for data management may inadvertently expose patient data to risks. This lack of knowledge can hinder the development of integrated healthcare solutions that benefit all parties involved, ultimately affecting patient care.

In the realm of real estate, ignorance about blockchain's impact on property transactions and ownership verification can lead to legal complications and financial losses. Blockchain technology can streamline the buying and selling process, ensuring more secure and efficient transactions. However, real estate professionals who are unaware of how to utilize smart contracts or maintain secure digital records may find themselves at a disadvantage in a rapidly evolving market. This gap in knowledge can lead to missed opportunities for innovation and growth in the industry.

Lastly, the risks associated with ignorance extend to the energy sector, where blockchain is reshaping renewable energy trading and distribution. Investors and companies that do not understand this technology may fail to capitalize on the potential for decentralized energy markets, which can provide significant cost savings and efficiency improvements. Additionally, a lack of awareness regarding blockchain's role in digital identity solutions can result in vulnerabilities in identity management and security. As various sectors continue to explore the benefits of blockchain, addressing the risks of ignorance is paramount for fostering a well-informed environment that encourages innovation and strategic growth.

The Importance of Continuous Learning

In the rapidly evolving landscape of blockchain technology, continuous learning emerges as a crucial component for investors, students, and professionals across various sectors. As we approach 2025, the implications of blockchain on industries such as financial services, supply chain management, healthcare, and more are becoming increasingly significant. The ability to understand these changes and adapt to new information is essential for making informed decisions. Continuous learning ensures that individuals and organizations can keep pace with advancements and leverage blockchain's potential while mitigating risks associated with its adoption.

For investors particularly, staying informed about the latest trends and developments in blockchain technology directly impacts investment strategies. The financial services sector is witnessing transformative changes due to blockchain's capability to enhance transparency, streamline processes, and reduce costs. Understanding the nuances of these changes is vital for making sound investment choices. Continuous learning allows investors to discern the advantages and disadvantages of blockchain applications, enabling them to navigate the associated challenges effectively. This knowledge is not only beneficial for maximizing returns but also for identifying potential pitfalls that could arise from technological disruptions.

In the realm of supply chain management, the push for transparency and efficiency is driving the adoption of blockchain. Stakeholders involved in logistics and distribution must continuously educate themselves about the benefits and challenges presented by this technology. Blockchain can provide enhanced traceability of products, ensuring authenticity and accountability. However, the integration of new systems poses risks, such as data security concerns and the need for widespread industry collaboration. By engaging in continuous learning, professionals in this field can better understand these dynamics and contribute to solutions that enhance supply chain resilience.

Healthcare is another sector where blockchain's implications are profound, particularly concerning patient data security and interoperability. Continuous learning about the intersection of blockchain and healthcare allows professionals to explore how decentralized systems can improve patient outcomes while protecting sensitive information. As regulations evolve and new technologies emerge, those involved in healthcare must stay abreast of these changes to implement effective strategies. This ongoing education fosters innovation and ensures that patient care remains at the forefront, addressing both ethical concerns and practical applications of blockchain.

Finally, the importance of continuous learning extends to the broader societal implications of blockchain, including its role in government, cybersecurity, digital identity, and beyond. As various sectors explore blockchain's potential for enhancing public records, voting systems, and digital identity solutions, the need for a well-informed populace becomes critical. Continuous learning equips individuals with the knowledge to engage in meaningful discussions about the pros and cons of blockchain adoption, encouraging a balanced approach to its implementation. This collective understanding will be vital in shaping policies and practices that harness blockchain's advantages while safeguarding against its vulnerabilities, ultimately fostering a more informed and resilient society in 2025 and beyond.

Chapter 3: Financial Services: Impact of Blockchain on Banking and Investment Strategies

Revolutionary Changes in Traditional Banking

The advent of blockchain technology has triggered revolutionary changes in traditional banking systems, fundamentally altering how financial institutions operate and interact with their customers. In 2025, this transformation is evident in various aspects of banking, from transaction processing to regulatory compliance. Traditional banks are no longer just custodians of money; they are evolving into technology-driven entities that seek to leverage the decentralized nature of blockchain to enhance efficiency, reduce costs, and improve customer trust. The integration of blockchain facilitates faster transaction times and lower fees, positioning banks to offer more competitive services in a landscape increasingly dominated by fintech innovations.

One of the most significant impacts of blockchain on traditional banking is the enhancement of transparency and security in transactions. Blockchain's immutable ledger provides an unprecedented level of accountability, allowing all parties involved in a transaction to verify its legitimacy without relying on a central authority. This transparency not only reduces the risk of fraud but also streamlines compliance processes. Banks are increasingly adopting smart contracts, which automate and enforce agreements, thus minimizing human error and potential disputes. As a result, the operational risk associated with traditional banking practices is significantly mitigated, allowing banks to focus on delivering better services to their clients.

Moreover, blockchain technology enables the democratization of financial services by facilitating access to banking for unbanked populations. In 2025, various blockchain-based platforms are emerging that allow individuals to conduct financial transactions without the need for traditional banking infrastructure. This shift is particularly impactful in developing regions, where access to banking services has historically been limited. By leveraging mobile technology and blockchain, these platforms are providing new opportunities for investment, savings, and credit, thereby fostering financial inclusion and stimulating economic growth.

However, the transition to a blockchain-based banking system is not without challenges. Traditional banks must navigate a complex regulatory landscape as they integrate blockchain technology into their operations. The lack of clear regulations can lead to uncertainty, making it difficult for banks to fully embrace blockchain innovations. Additionally, there are concerns about cybersecurity, as the adoption of new technologies may introduce vulnerabilities that could be exploited by malicious actors. Banks must invest in robust security measures to protect against potential threats, balancing innovation with the need to safeguard sensitive customer information.

As we look towards the future, the relationship between traditional banking and blockchain technology will continue to evolve. Investors and stakeholders in the financial sector must stay informed about the ongoing developments and the strategic implications of this transformation. Understanding the pros and cons of blockchain in banking is essential for formulating effective investment strategies and making informed decisions. As traditional banks adapt to this new landscape, they will have to embrace a culture of innovation, ensuring that they remain competitive and relevant in an increasingly digital world.

Investment Strategies Enhanced by Blockchain

Investment strategies are evolving rapidly as blockchain technology continues to reshape various sectors. Investors are increasingly recognizing the potential of blockchain to enhance traditional investment approaches, particularly in financial services. The decentralized nature of blockchain offers transparency and security, which can significantly reduce risks associated with fraud and mismanagement. Moreover, investment strategies that leverage blockchain facilitate real-time data access and analysis, enabling investors to make more informed decisions. As financial institutions adopt blockchain for operations such as cross-border payments and asset tokenization, investors must understand how these innovations can optimize their portfolios.

In the realm of supply chain management, blockchain introduces a new level of transparency that can greatly benefit investors. By providing a tamper-proof record of transactions, blockchain allows stakeholders to trace the provenance of goods and verify authenticity. This transparency can mitigate risks associated with counterfeit products and inefficiencies in logistics. Investors in supply chain-focused companies can leverage blockchain's capabilities to evaluate the operational integrity of their investments, ensuring that they are backing businesses that prioritize accountability and ethical practices.

Healthcare is another sector where blockchain has profound implications for investment strategies. With patient data security being paramount, blockchain provides a means to secure sensitive information while promoting interoperability among healthcare providers. Investments in healthcare tech companies that utilize blockchain for electronic health records can lead to more efficient patient care and reduced healthcare costs. Understanding the potential for blockchain to enhance data security and streamline operations can help investors identify promising opportunities in this rapidly growing market.

The real estate industry is also experiencing a transformation through blockchain technology. By facilitating smart contracts and automating property transactions, blockchain minimizes the need for intermediaries, thereby reducing costs and expediting processes. Investors can benefit from more straightforward ownership verification and a reduction in fraud associated with property transactions. The ability to tokenize real estate assets further opens up investment opportunities, allowing for fractional ownership and broader access to real estate markets. As these innovations gain traction, investors should consider how blockchain can enhance their real estate portfolios.

Lastly, the implications of blockchain for digital identity present both opportunities and challenges for investors. As organizations explore blockchain-based identity solutions, the potential for enhanced security and privacy increases. However, concerns regarding data breaches and the permanence of blockchain records must be addressed. Investors should evaluate companies that prioritize robust security measures and regulatory compliance in their blockchain identity offerings. By understanding the balance between innovation and security, investors can make strategic decisions in a landscape that is constantly evolving due to advancements in blockchain technology.

Challenges in Adoption by Financial Institutions

Financial institutions face numerous challenges in adopting blockchain technology, which can hinder their ability to leverage its potential benefits. One significant issue is regulatory uncertainty. As blockchain technology evolves, so do the regulatory frameworks surrounding it. Financial institutions must navigate inconsistent regulations across jurisdictions and adapt to changing compliance requirements. This uncertainty creates apprehension among banks and investment firms, which are often risk-averse by nature, leading to delays in the adoption of innovative technologies that could enhance efficiency and security.

Another challenge lies in the integration of blockchain with existing legacy systems. Many financial institutions operate on outdated infrastructure that is not designed to accommodate new technologies. The process of integrating blockchain solutions with these systems can be complex and costly, requiring substantial investment in both time and resources. Institutions must also consider the potential disruption to operations during the transition period, which can further complicate the decision to adopt blockchain technology.

Security and privacy concerns also play a pivotal role in the reluctance of financial institutions to adopt blockchain. Despite its reputation for enhanced security features, blockchain is not immune to vulnerabilities. Cybersecurity threats, such as hacking and data breaches, can undermine trust in blockchain solutions. Additionally, the transparent nature of many blockchain applications raises concerns about the privacy of sensitive financial data. Financial institutions must carefully assess these risks and implement robust security measures to protect their clients' information while leveraging the benefits of blockchain technology.

Moreover, the skills gap presents a significant barrier to blockchain adoption within financial institutions. As the technology continues to evolve, there is a growing demand for professionals with expertise in blockchain development, implementation, and maintenance. Many traditional financial institutions struggle to attract and retain talent in this area, resulting in a shortage of qualified personnel to drive blockchain initiatives forward. This skills gap can stall progress and prevent organizations from fully understanding and capitalizing on blockchain's potential.

Lastly, the fragmentation of the blockchain ecosystem poses challenges for financial institutions seeking to adopt the technology. With various blockchain platforms and protocols available, institutions may find it difficult to identify which solutions best align with their strategic goals. This fragmentation can lead to uncertainty about interoperability between different blockchain networks, affecting the seamless exchange of information and assets. Financial institutions must carefully navigate this landscape to select the appropriate blockchain solutions that can work effectively within their operations while considering collaboration with other stakeholders in the ecosystem.

Chapter 4: Supply Chain Management: Benefits and Challenges of Transparency in Logistics

Enhancing Transparency and Traceability

Enhancing transparency and traceability is a pivotal advantage of blockchain technology that resonates across various sectors, particularly in 2025. For investors and corporations, this characteristic fosters a more trustworthy environment, crucial for making informed decisions. In financial services, for instance, blockchain enables real-time access to transaction histories, which can significantly reduce fraud and errors in banking and investment strategies. By providing a clear audit trail, organizations can validate the authenticity of transactions and enhance compliance with regulatory requirements, thereby increasing investor confidence and participation in the market.

In supply chain management, transparency and traceability offered by blockchain are transformative. Stakeholders can track products from origin to destination, ensuring accountability at every stage of the supply chain. This capability not only enhances the efficiency of logistics but also mitigates risks associated with counterfeit goods and ethical sourcing. By leveraging blockchain, companies can provide consumers with verifiable information about the products they purchase, leading to more informed consumer choices and fostering brand loyalty. However, challenges such as the integration of blockchain with existing systems and the need for industry-wide collaboration can hinder its widespread adoption.

The healthcare sector stands to benefit immensely from blockchain's transparency, particularly concerning patient data security and interoperability. By utilizing blockchain, healthcare providers can maintain accurate and immutable records of patient information, thus facilitating seamless data sharing among authorized entities. This capability not only improves the quality of care but also enhances patient privacy and control over their own data. Nevertheless, the implementation of blockchain in healthcare must navigate complex regulatory environments and concerns about data ownership, which can complicate its integration into existing healthcare systems.

In real estate, blockchain enhances property transactions and ownership verification, streamlining processes that have traditionally been cumbersome and prone to fraud. By recording property titles on a blockchain, stakeholders can ensure a transparent and tamper-proof record of ownership, which simplifies the buying and selling process. Furthermore, blockchain can facilitate smart contracts that automate and enforce agreements without the need for intermediaries. However, the legal recognition of blockchain-based transactions and the potential for technological obsolescence remain significant hurdles that need to be addressed.

Lastly, the role of blockchain in education, particularly for credential verification and academic records, exemplifies its potential for enhancing transparency. Institutions can utilize blockchain to issue digital diplomas and certificates that are easily verifiable by employers, thereby reducing the risk of credential fraud. This not only benefits graduates by enhancing their employability but also assists employers in making informed hiring decisions. While the advantages are clear, the education sector must also contend with issues of data privacy and the need for standardized practices to ensure that blockchain solutions are effective and widely accepted.

Reducing Costs and Increasing Efficiency

Reducing costs and increasing efficiency through blockchain technology is a compelling prospect for various sectors, particularly in 2025. For investors, understanding the financial implications of adopting blockchain can lead to significant cost savings and operational efficiencies. In the financial services sector, blockchain provides a decentralized ledger that simplifies transactions between parties, eliminates the need for intermediaries, and reduces transaction fees. As banks and investment firms integrate blockchain into their operations, they gain access to faster processing times and enhanced transparency, ultimately leading to a more streamlined financial ecosystem.

In supply chain management, blockchain enables real-time tracking and verification of goods as they move through the logistics chain. This transparency helps reduce fraud, errors, and inefficiencies, allowing companies to lower operational costs. By employing smart contracts, organizations can automate various processes, such as payment releases upon delivery confirmation, thereby minimizing delays and human error. As a result, companies can optimize inventory levels and improve customer satisfaction, creating a more resilient and cost-effective supply chain.

The healthcare industry stands to benefit significantly from blockchain's potential to enhance patient data security and interoperability. By creating a secure and immutable record of patient information, healthcare providers can reduce administrative costs associated with data management and retrieval. Furthermore, blockchain can facilitate seamless data sharing among providers, thereby enhancing care coordination and reducing duplication of services. In turn, improved data integrity can lead to better patient outcomes and lower healthcare costs, making it an attractive investment area.

In the realm of real estate, blockchain has the potential to transform property transactions and ownership verification. Traditional processes often involve extensive paperwork and multiple intermediaries, leading to increased costs and time delays. By utilizing blockchain for title management and transaction recording, parties can achieve a more efficient transfer of ownership, significantly reducing closing costs and timeframes. This shift not only benefits investors but also enhances buyer confidence and market liquidity, making real estate investments more appealing.

Lastly, blockchain's applications in education, government, cybersecurity, and the energy sector present additional avenues for cost reduction and efficiency gains. In education, blockchain can streamline credential verification processes, reducing administrative burdens and enhancing trust in academic records. Governments can use blockchain for public records and voting systems, improving transparency and reducing the risk of fraud. In cybersecurity, while there are vulnerabilities to consider, blockchain's security features can strengthen data protection, mitigating costs associated with breaches. Similarly, in the energy sector, blockchain can facilitate peer-to-peer energy trading, reducing costs and enhancing efficiency in renewable energy distribution. Each of these sectors illustrates how understanding and leveraging blockchain technology can lead to significant improvements in cost management and operational efficiency.

Potential Pitfalls in Supply Chain Implementation

Potential pitfalls in supply chain implementation of blockchain technology encompass several critical areas that investors and stakeholders must navigate carefully. One of the foremost challenges is the integration of blockchain with existing systems and processes. Many organizations have invested heavily in legacy systems that may not easily interface with new blockchain solutions. This can lead to increased costs and extended timelines as companies seek to harmonize disparate technologies. Furthermore, the complexity of implementing blockchain across a global supply chain can introduce operational disruptions, particularly if there is insufficient training or understanding among personnel about how to utilize the new technology effectively.

Data privacy and security concerns also play a significant role in the potential pitfalls of blockchain in supply chain management. While blockchain is often lauded for its security features, the immutability of recorded data can pose risks when sensitive information is involved. If confidential business data or proprietary information is stored on a blockchain, the lack of flexibility to alter or delete that data can expose organizations to vulnerabilities. This is particularly pertinent in industries like healthcare and finance, where data breaches could have severe consequences. Stakeholders must weigh the benefits of transparency against the need for confidentiality and data protection.

Another potential pitfall is the regulatory landscape surrounding blockchain technology. As governments and regulatory bodies continue to develop frameworks for blockchain applications, uncertainty can arise regarding compliance and legal implications. Investors and corporations may find it challenging to navigate this evolving regulatory environment, leading to potential delays in implementation or unforeseen liabilities. Additionally, differing regulations across jurisdictions can complicate international supply chain operations, as companies must ensure they are compliant with multiple sets of rules and standards.

Interoperability is a critical concern in blockchain supply chain initiatives. For blockchain to achieve its full potential in enhancing transparency and efficiency, it must be able to communicate seamlessly across various platforms and systems. Lack of standardization in blockchain protocols can hinder this interoperability, resulting in fragmented systems that fail to deliver the promised benefits of real-time data sharing and visibility. Investors should remain cautious about the viability of blockchain solutions that do not prioritize or facilitate interoperability with other technologies and networks.

Lastly, the human element cannot be overlooked in the implementation of blockchain within supply chains. Resistance to change, insufficient skilled talent, and lack of stakeholder engagement can undermine even the most well-planned blockchain initiatives. Organizations must invest in change management strategies and training programs to ensure that all employees understand the benefits and functionalities of blockchain. Without buy-in from all levels of the organization, the potential advantages of blockchain in supply chain management may not be fully realized, leading to wasted resources and missed opportunities.

Chapter 5: Healthcare: Implications of Blockchain for Patient Data Security and Interoperability

Securing Patient Data with Blockchain

Securing patient data has become a paramount concern in the healthcare industry, especially as digital transformation accelerates and cyber threats evolve. Blockchain technology offers a promising solution to enhance data security and integrity. By decentralizing data storage and using cryptographic methods, blockchain can protect sensitive patient information from unauthorized access and tampering. Each transaction or data entry is recorded in a secure, immutable ledger, ensuring that patient records are not only protected but also traceable. This capability is crucial for healthcare providers who must comply with stringent regulations such as HIPAA while maintaining patient trust.

One of the primary benefits of using blockchain for patient data security is the enhancement of data interoperability. Traditional systems often suffer from silos, where patient information is fragmented across various platforms, making it challenging to access comprehensive health records. Blockchain facilitates a unified approach, allowing various healthcare entities to access a single, verified source of patient data. This interoperability can lead to improved patient care, as healthcare professionals have access to accurate and up-to-date information, reducing the risk of errors and enhancing treatment outcomes.

Moreover, the transparency inherent in blockchain technology can play a significant role in auditing and compliance. Every transaction is timestamped and recorded, providing a clear audit trail that can be invaluable during compliance checks. Healthcare organizations can quickly demonstrate adherence to data protection regulations, thereby minimizing the risk of penalties. This level of transparency also empowers patients, who can have greater control over their own data and can choose who accesses their information, fostering a sense of autonomy and trust in the healthcare system.

However, while the potential benefits of blockchain in securing patient data are substantial, there are also challenges and limitations to consider. The implementation of blockchain technology can be complex and costly, requiring significant investment in infrastructure and training. Additionally, the scalability of blockchain solutions remains a concern, particularly in an industry that generates vast amounts of data daily. Healthcare organizations must weigh these factors against the potential advantages, considering both the short-term costs and long-term gains.

As the healthcare sector continues to explore the application of blockchain for patient data security, collaboration among stakeholders is essential. Investors, tech companies, and healthcare providers must work together to develop standards and best practices that ensure effective implementation. By fostering a cooperative environment, the industry can navigate the challenges associated with integrating blockchain technology, ultimately leading to improved patient data security and enhancing the overall healthcare experience.

Interoperability Challenges and Solutions

Interoperability challenges in blockchain technology present significant barriers to its widespread adoption across various sectors, including finance, healthcare, and supply chain management. Different blockchain networks often operate in silos, each with unique protocols and standards. This lack of standardization complicates data sharing and transaction processing among systems, leading to inefficiencies and increased operational costs. For investors and organizations seeking to leverage blockchain solutions, understanding these interoperability challenges is crucial, as they can impact the scalability and functionality of blockchain applications.

One of the most pressing interoperability issues lies in the diverse consensus mechanisms employed by various blockchain platforms. For instance, some networks utilize proof of work, while others adopt proof of stake or delegated proof of stake. Each consensus approach has its own benefits and drawbacks, which can hinder seamless communication between different blockchains. As a result, organizations must consider the compatibility of their chosen blockchain solutions with existing systems and evaluate how these differences may affect their operations. Investors should be aware that projects addressing interoperability are gaining traction, which may present viable investment opportunities.

Several solutions are emerging to tackle interoperability challenges within the blockchain landscape. Cross-chain technology, such as atomic swaps and interoperability protocols like Polkadot and Cosmos, enables different blockchain networks to communicate and exchange data securely. These solutions are designed to facilitate transactions and information sharing without compromising the integrity of individual blockchains. For investors, understanding these technologies and their potential to bridge gaps between platforms can provide insight into the future direction of blockchain applications across various industries.

Another promising approach to enhancing interoperability is the development of industry-specific standards. Collaborative efforts among stakeholders—ranging from corporations to regulatory bodies—can lead to the establishment of common frameworks that promote seamless integration between different blockchain networks. For example, the healthcare sector could benefit from standardized protocols that ensure patient data can be securely shared among various providers while maintaining compliance with regulations such as HIPAA. Investors should monitor these initiatives, as they may influence the success and adoption rates of blockchain solutions in specific markets.

In conclusion, addressing interoperability challenges is essential for the realization of blockchain's full potential across various sectors. While the current landscape presents significant hurdles, ongoing technological advancements and collaborative standardization efforts offer promising pathways to overcome these barriers. Investors, tech industry professionals, and academic institutions must stay informed about these developments to capitalize on the opportunities that arise from a more interconnected blockchain ecosystem. Understanding and navigating these challenges will ultimately determine the success of blockchain implementations in enhancing efficiency and transparency across industries.

The Future of Healthcare Data Management

The future of healthcare data management is poised for transformation with the integration of blockchain technology, which offers a decentralized approach to secure patient data. In 2025, healthcare stakeholders including investors, technology companies, and academic institutions will need to understand the implications of blockchain for data security and interoperability. By leveraging blockchain's cryptographic features, healthcare organizations can enhance the security of sensitive patient information, reducing the risk of data breaches and unauthorized access. This technology allows for the creation of immutable records that ensure data integrity, thereby fostering greater trust among patients and providers.

Interoperability remains a significant challenge in healthcare, as disparate systems often hinder the seamless exchange of patient information. Blockchain presents a solution by providing a common framework for data sharing across different platforms while maintaining privacy and consent protocols. In 2025, we can expect a growing emphasis on the development of blockchain-based solutions that facilitate interoperability, enabling healthcare providers to access comprehensive patient histories without compromising data security. This shift could lead to improved patient outcomes and more efficient care delivery, positioning blockchain as a vital component of future healthcare ecosystems.

Furthermore, the potential for blockchain to streamline administrative processes in healthcare cannot be overlooked. By automating tasks such as billing, claims processing, and patient consent management through smart contracts, healthcare organizations can reduce operational costs and minimize human error. Investors looking to capitalize on this trend should focus on startups and established companies that are developing innovative blockchain solutions aimed at enhancing operational efficiency. The adoption of these technologies will likely result in significant cost savings and improved resource allocation, making them attractive investment opportunities in the evolving healthcare landscape.

Despite the promise that blockchain holds, it is essential to recognize the challenges associated with its implementation in healthcare. The complexity of integrating blockchain with existing systems can pose significant barriers to entry, particularly for smaller organizations that may lack the necessary resources. Additionally, regulatory uncertainties surrounding data privacy laws, such as HIPAA in the United States, could hinder the widespread adoption of blockchain solutions. Investors and stakeholders must remain informed about these challenges and assess the viability of blockchain initiatives within the healthcare sector carefully.

Ultimately, the future of healthcare data management will be shaped by the ongoing dialogue between technological innovation and regulatory frameworks. As blockchain technology matures, its role in enhancing patient data security and interoperability will become increasingly important. Investors, corporations, and academic institutions must collaborate to navigate the complexities of this landscape, ensuring that blockchain's potential is harnessed effectively. The proactive engagement of various stakeholders will be crucial in addressing the challenges and maximizing the benefits of blockchain in healthcare, setting the stage for a more secure and efficient system in the years to come.

Chapter 6: Real Estate: How Blockchain Affects Property Transactions and Ownership Verification

Streamlining Property Transactions

Streamlining property transactions through blockchain technology offers significant advantages that can transform the real estate market. Traditional property transactions often involve lengthy processes, numerous intermediaries, and extensive paperwork, leading to delays and increased costs. By leveraging blockchain, these transactions can be expedited through a decentralized ledger that securely records all ownership transfers and relevant property information. This technology ensures that all parties involved have access to the same information in real-time, significantly reducing the time required to complete transactions and enhancing the overall efficiency of the process.

One of the primary benefits of blockchain in property transactions is the improvement in ownership verification. The use of smart contracts on blockchain platforms allows for automated execution of agreements once predetermined conditions are met. This eliminates the need for intermediaries, such as notaries and title companies, who traditionally verify ownership and validate property titles. By providing a transparent and immutable record of property ownership, blockchain technology minimizes the risk of fraud and ensures that buyers can trust the legitimacy of the transactions they are engaging in, thus fostering greater confidence in the real estate market.

Additionally, blockchain can enhance the accessibility of property transaction data. This is especially valuable for investors, as it allows for a more informed decision-making process. With a reliable and publicly accessible record of property transactions, potential buyers can easily trace the history of a property, including previous ownerships and any liens or claims against it. This level of transparency not only benefits individual investors but also enhances market stability by providing all stakeholders with the information necessary to assess the value and risks associated with real estate investments.

Despite its advantages, the implementation of blockchain in property transactions also presents challenges. The transition from traditional systems to blockchain-based solutions requires significant investment in technology infrastructure and regulatory adjustments. Furthermore, there is a need for widespread acceptance among industry stakeholders, including real estate professionals, government bodies, and financial institutions. Ensuring that all parties are equipped with the knowledge and tools to navigate this new landscape is crucial for the successful integration of blockchain into property transactions.

In conclusion, while the streamlining of property transactions through blockchain technology presents numerous benefits, it also necessitates careful consideration of the challenges involved. For investors and industry participants, understanding both the potential and the limitations of blockchain in real estate is vital to making informed decisions. As the technology continues to evolve, its ability to enhance efficiency, security, and transparency will likely shape the future of property transactions and ownership verification, making it an essential area of focus for those navigating the blockchain landscape in 2025.

Ensuring Ownership Verification

Ensuring ownership verification is a critical aspect of blockchain technology that resonates across various sectors, particularly in real estate. The decentralized nature of blockchain provides a unique solution to the longstanding issues of property fraud and title disputes. By recording ownership on an immutable ledger, stakeholders can access transparent and verifiable data regarding property titles. This digital approach not only enhances trust among investors and buyers but also simplifies the process of transferring property ownership. As investors navigate the intricacies of blockchain in 2025, understanding how ownership verification functions within this framework is paramount for making informed decisions.

The benefits of blockchain for ownership verification extend beyond mere transparency. Traditional systems often rely on cumbersome paperwork and multiple intermediaries, which can lead to inefficiencies and increased costs. With blockchain, every transaction is recorded in real-time, allowing for quick and efficient verification of ownership. This efficiency reduces the potential for errors and fraud, ultimately fostering a safer investment environment. Investors, corporations, and educational institutions can leverage this technology to ensure that assets, whether physical properties or digital credentials, are authenticated and secure.

However, the implementation of blockchain for ownership verification also presents challenges that must be addressed. One significant concern is the need for widespread adoption of blockchain standards across different jurisdictions. Without a unified approach, discrepancies may arise in how ownership is recorded and verified, leading to confusion and potential legal disputes. Moreover, the transition from traditional systems to blockchain requires substantial investment in infrastructure and education. Stakeholders must weigh these challenges against the potential gains in efficiency, security, and trust that blockchain promises.

In sectors like healthcare and supply chain management, the implications of ownership verification can also be profound. For instance, patient data security hinges on the accurate verification of data ownership and access rights. Blockchain can facilitate this by ensuring that only authorized individuals have access to sensitive information, thus enhancing patient privacy and compliance with regulations. Similarly, in supply chain scenarios, verifying ownership of goods at each stage can improve accountability and reduce the risk of fraud, ultimately leading to a more reliable logistics system.

As blockchain technology continues to evolve, its role in ownership verification will likely expand across various industries. Investors must stay informed about both the opportunities and challenges that come with this digital revolution. By understanding how to navigate ownership verification through blockchain, stakeholders can better position themselves to take advantage of the efficiencies and security enhancements offered by this innovative technology. The future of ownership verification in 2025 is poised to transform the way assets are managed and transferred, making it an essential area of focus for anyone involved in investment and asset management.

Regulatory Challenges in Real Estate Blockchain

Regulatory challenges in the real estate sector are becoming increasingly complex as blockchain technology continues to gain traction. One of the primary issues is the lack of a unified regulatory framework that specifically addresses blockchain applications in real estate transactions. Different jurisdictions have varying interpretations of existing laws and regulations, which can lead to confusion for investors and developers alike. This inconsistency raises questions about compliance and the legitimacy of blockchain-based property transactions, making it essential for stakeholders to remain informed about the legal landscape in their respective regions.

Another significant challenge involves the integration of blockchain technology with existing legal frameworks governing property rights and ownership. Traditional real estate transactions are heavily regulated, with established processes for title transfers, disclosures, and record-keeping. The introduction of blockchain could disrupt these established practices, as it enables decentralized ownership records, which may not align with current laws. Investors and real estate professionals must navigate these regulatory hurdles to ensure that blockchain implementations do not violate existing statutes, potentially leading to legal disputes or regulatory penalties.

Privacy and data protection also pose regulatory challenges in the context of real estate blockchain. The decentralized nature of blockchain means that transaction data is often publicly accessible, raising concerns about the confidentiality of sensitive information. This is particularly critical in real estate, where details about property ownership and transactions can impact market dynamics. Investors must be aware of the implications of data privacy laws, such as the General Data Protection Regulation (GDPR) in Europe, which could affect how blockchain solutions are designed and implemented to protect personal information.

Moreover, the potential for fraud and misuse of blockchain in real estate transactions presents a regulatory concern. While blockchain technology is often touted for its security features, it is not immune to vulnerabilities. For instance, if smart contracts are poorly coded or if there are flaws in the underlying blockchain infrastructure, it could lead to unauthorized access or manipulation of property records. Regulators need to establish guidelines to enhance security measures and enforce accountability among blockchain developers and users, ensuring that the technology is used responsibly and effectively.

Lastly, the evolving nature of blockchain technology itself poses a challenge for regulators. As new innovations emerge, such as tokenization of real estate assets and decentralized finance (DeFi) applications, regulatory bodies must adapt to these changes to provide adequate oversight. This requires ongoing collaboration between industry stakeholders and regulators to foster an environment that encourages innovation while protecting investors and ensuring compliance. For investors and professionals in the real estate sector, understanding these regulatory challenges is crucial for navigating the complexities of blockchain technology in property transactions effectively.

Chapter 7: Education: The Role of Blockchain in Credential Verification and Academic Records

Enhancing Credential Verification Processes

Enhancing credential verification processes through blockchain technology presents a transformative opportunity for various sectors, particularly in education and employment. Traditional methods of verifying academic achievements and professional qualifications are often cumbersome, prone to errors, and susceptible to fraud. By leveraging blockchain, institutions can create immutable records that are easily verifiable, allowing employers and educational bodies to access accurate information quickly. This not only streamlines hiring processes but also enhances trust in the credentials presented by candidates. The decentralized nature of blockchain provides a secure environment for storing these records, significantly reducing the risk of data tampering.

In the education sector, blockchain can facilitate the issuance of digital diplomas and certificates that are linked to a student's unique digital identity. This innovation empowers students to take control of their academic records and share them selectively with prospective employers or institutions. Additionally, blockchain enables the creation of a transparent ledger where all educational achievements are recorded in real-time. This level of transparency not only makes it easier for employers to verify qualifications but also helps educational institutions maintain their integrity and credibility by reducing the chances of diploma mills and fraudulent claims.

Furthermore, integrating blockchain into credential verification can address the complexities involved in cross-institutional recognition of qualifications. As globalization increases, students and professionals often seek opportunities across borders. Blockchain technology can facilitate the standardization of credential verification processes, ensuring that qualifications are recognized and trusted internationally. This can significantly enhance mobility for students and professionals alike, fostering a more interconnected global workforce. The potential for real-time updates to records also means that any new qualifications or achievements can be instantly reflected on an individual's blockchain profile.

However, the implementation of blockchain for credential verification is not without its challenges. Organizations must navigate the technical complexities of integrating blockchain with existing systems, which can require substantial investment and training. Moreover, issues related to data privacy and consent must be addressed to ensure that individuals have control over their own information. Regulatory frameworks around the use of blockchain for educational and employment verification are still in development, which can create uncertainty for institutions looking to adopt this technology. Therefore, stakeholders must engage in collaborative efforts to create compliant and user-friendly systems that prioritize both security and accessibility.

In conclusion, enhancing credential verification processes through blockchain technology holds significant promise for improving the efficiency and reliability of academic and professional qualifications. By providing a secure, transparent, and easily accessible means of verifying credentials, blockchain can reduce fraudulent claims and streamline verification processes across various sectors. As stakeholders collaborate to address the challenges of implementation, the potential benefits for investors, educational institutions, corporations, and individuals will continue to expand, shaping the future of credential verification in an increasingly digital world.

Protecting Academic Records from Fraud

Academic records have long been a target for fraud, with counterfeit diplomas and transcripts posing significant challenges for educational institutions and employers alike. The emergence of blockchain technology offers a promising solution to these longstanding issues. By utilizing a decentralized and immutable ledger, educational institutions can store academic records securely, ensuring that they are tamper-proof and easily verifiable. Blockchain can provide a transparent and trustworthy framework for credential verification, allowing students to share their qualifications with prospective employers confidently, while significantly reducing the risk of fraud.

One of the critical advantages of blockchain in protecting academic records is its inherent transparency. Each transaction or update made to the blockchain is recorded in a way that is visible to all participants in the network. This feature can discourage fraudulent activities, as any attempt to alter or falsify records would be immediately detectable. Additionally, the use of cryptographic techniques further enhances data security, ensuring that only authorized users can access or modify sensitive information. Educational institutions can thus maintain the integrity of academic records, fostering greater trust in the qualifications of their graduates.

Moreover, the implementation of blockchain technology can streamline the process of credential verification for employers. Currently, verifying academic qualifications often involves lengthy procedures, including contacting institutions and waiting for confirmation. Blockchain can expedite this process by providing a real-time, digital verification system where employers can directly access and verify an applicant's credentials on the blockchain. This efficiency not only saves time for employers but also enhances the employment prospects of graduates, as they can readily prove their qualifications without the risk of fraudulent claims.

However, the integration of blockchain into academic record keeping is not without its challenges. Educational institutions must navigate technical, regulatory, and financial considerations before adopting this technology. The initial setup costs and the need for specialized knowledge can be significant barriers, particularly for smaller institutions. Furthermore, there are concerns about data privacy and compliance with existing regulations, such as the Family

Educational Rights and Privacy Act (FERPA) in the United States, which protects student information. Balancing transparency with privacy will be a crucial aspect of developing a successful blockchain-based system for academic records.

In conclusion, while the adoption of blockchain technology in education presents significant opportunities for enhancing the security and integrity of academic records, it also necessitates a careful consideration of the associated challenges. As investors, educators, and tech industry leaders evaluate the potential of blockchain for credential verification, it is essential to stay informed about the evolving landscape. By understanding both the benefits and the obstacles, stakeholders can make informed decisions that advance the protection of academic records while fostering innovation and trust in the educational system.

Future Trends in Educational Blockchain Applications

The integration of blockchain technology in education is poised for significant evolution in the coming years. One of the most promising applications is in the realm of credential verification. As educational institutions increasingly recognize the importance of authenticating academic records, blockchain's decentralized and immutable nature offers a reliable solution. This not only streamlines the verification process for employers and educational institutions but also reduces fraud and enhances trust in credentials. As adoption grows, we can expect to see a wider range of institutions participating in blockchain networks, ultimately leading to a more standardized and efficient credentialing system.

Another emerging trend is the use of blockchain for personalized learning experiences. By leveraging smart contracts, educational institutions can create customized learning pathways that adapt to individual students' needs and progress. This approach allows for more flexible curricula, enabling students to acquire skills at their own pace. As educational content becomes more modular and accessible, the ability to track and validate learning achievements on a blockchain will empower both students and educators to engage in more meaningful educational interactions. This shift could lead to a transformation in how educational success is measured and recognized.

Furthermore, blockchain technology has the potential to facilitate micro-credentialing and lifelong learning. As the job market rapidly evolves, the demand for continuous skill development is becoming paramount. Blockchain can support the issuance of micro-credentials that represent specific skills or competencies acquired through various learning experiences. These digital badges or certificates can be easily shared and verified, providing a dynamic record of an individual's professional development. This trend not only encourages lifelong learning but also enables employers to assess candidates based on specific skills rather than solely on traditional degrees.

The role of blockchain in enhancing collaboration between educational institutions and industry partners is also set to expand. By creating transparent and secure channels for data sharing, blockchain can enhance partnerships that focus on workforce readiness and skill alignment. Companies can access real-time data regarding the competencies of graduates, allowing them to tailor their training programs and recruitment strategies. This collaboration could lead to more effective educational outcomes, bridging the gap between academia and industry, and equipping students with the relevant skills needed in the workforce.

Lastly, the potential for blockchain to revolutionize funding and financial aid systems in education cannot be overlooked. By facilitating transparent and efficient transactions, blockchain can streamline processes such as student loans, scholarships, and grants. This increased transparency can help to reduce fraud and ensure that funds are allocated appropriately. As educational institutions explore innovative funding models, the integration of blockchain could lead to more equitable access to education and resources for students from diverse backgrounds, ultimately shaping a more inclusive educational landscape.

Chapter 8: Government: Pros and Cons of Using Blockchain for Public Records and Voting Systems

Improving Transparency in Public Records

Improving transparency in public records through blockchain technology presents a significant opportunity for various sectors, particularly in enhancing trust and accountability. By utilizing a decentralized ledger system, government entities can ensure that public records are immutable, verifiable, and accessible to all stakeholders. This process mitigates risks associated with data tampering and unauthorized access, thus fostering public confidence in the integrity of governmental operations. Investors and corporations alike stand to benefit from increased transparency, as it can lead to more efficient decision-making and reduced costs associated with compliance and audits.

In financial services, the application of blockchain technology to public records can streamline banking and investment strategies. With transparent and traceable records, financial institutions can verify the authenticity of transactions in real-time, reducing the risk of fraud and enhancing regulatory compliance. This newfound transparency can also facilitate smoother audits, enabling investors to conduct thorough due diligence with greater ease. As a result, the financial sector can offer more reliable products and services, ultimately leading to improved investor confidence and market stability.

Supply chain management is another area poised for transformation through enhanced transparency in public records. Blockchain enables the tracking of goods from origin to destination, providing stakeholders with real-time visibility into the logistics process. This transparency can address issues related to product authenticity and provenance, which are crucial for industries such as food and pharmaceuticals. By improving record-keeping and traceability, companies can not only comply with regulatory requirements but also enhance their reputations and consumer trust, leading to a more resilient supply chain.

In healthcare, blockchain can revolutionize patient data security and interoperability by creating transparent and secure records. Patients can have full control over their health data, granting access to providers as needed while ensuring their privacy is protected. This transparency can lead to improved patient outcomes, as healthcare professionals can access comprehensive and accurate information. Additionally, the ability to audit access and modifications to medical records can help protect against data breaches, thus enhancing the overall security of sensitive information in the healthcare system.

The implications of blockchain for public records extend to various sectors, including real estate, education, and government. In real estate, blockchain can simplify property transactions by providing transparent ownership records, reducing disputes, and streamlining the transfer process. In education, it can enhance the verification of academic credentials, ensuring that qualifications are easily accessible and verifiable. Governments can leverage blockchain to improve public records management and voting systems, making processes more transparent and efficient. Overall, as organizations and institutions embrace blockchain technology, the potential for improved transparency in public records can lead to significant advancements across multiple domains.

Enhancing Election Security and Integrity

Enhancing election security and integrity through blockchain technology presents a compelling opportunity for improving democratic processes. As concerns about election interference and fraud continue to loom, the immutable and transparent nature of blockchain offers a potential solution. By recording votes on a decentralized ledger, each transaction becomes verifiable and traceable, reducing the risk of tampering. This system can help ensure that every vote counts and that election outcomes are accurate, fostering public trust in democratic institutions.

One of the primary advantages of utilizing blockchain in elections is the potential for increased voter participation. Traditional voting methods often involve cumbersome processes that can deter voters, especially those in remote areas. Blockchain can facilitate remote voting through secure digital platforms, allowing individuals to cast their ballots conveniently. This accessibility could lead to higher turnout rates, reflecting a more representative electorate and ultimately enhancing the legitimacy of election results.

However, the integration of blockchain into electoral systems is not without challenges. Concerns regarding cybersecurity remain paramount; while blockchain provides a robust framework, it is not immune to hacking. A breach in the system could undermine the very integrity it aims to protect. Therefore, it is critical for stakeholders, including governments and tech companies, to invest in comprehensive security measures and protocols to safeguard these systems against potential vulnerabilities and ensure that they remain resilient against evolving threats.

Moreover, the implementation of blockchain technology in elections raises important questions about digital identity verification. Ensuring that each voter is who they claim to be is essential to prevent fraud. While blockchain can help create secure digital identities, it poses challenges related to privacy and data protection. Striking the right balance between transparency and confidentiality is crucial to maintaining public trust and ensuring that sensitive information is adequately protected.

Finally, the move toward blockchain-based election systems necessitates a collaborative effort among various sectors, including government, tech industries, and educational institutions. These entities must work together to develop standards and best practices that address the multifaceted implications of this technology. By fostering an environment of innovation and cooperation, stakeholders can harness the benefits of blockchain, paving the way for a more secure and trustworthy electoral process that aligns with the expectations of modern society.

Challenges of Implementing Blockchain in Government

The implementation of blockchain technology in government presents a range of challenges that can complicate its adoption and effectiveness. One of the primary hurdles is the existing regulatory framework. Governments operate within established laws and regulations that may not readily accommodate the decentralized and often anonymous nature of blockchain. Adjusting these frameworks to align with the principles of blockchain, while ensuring compliance with public accountability and transparency, requires significant legal and bureaucratic changes. This process can be slow and contentious, as stakeholders debate the implications of shifting from traditional systems to decentralized models.

Another challenge is the need for technological infrastructure. Many governments lack the necessary technical capabilities and infrastructure to support blockchain systems effectively. Upgrading existing systems to integrate blockchain technology can be costly and time-consuming. Additionally, there is often a skills gap within government agencies, as personnel may not possess the expertise required to implement and manage blockchain solutions. Training and recruiting skilled professionals in this space are essential, but they also demand investment and commitment from government entities.

Interoperability poses another significant challenge. For blockchain to be effective in government applications, it must work seamlessly with existing systems and technologies. This requires establishing standards and protocols that can facilitate communication between various blockchain networks and traditional databases. The absence of universally accepted standards can lead to fragmentation, where different agencies adopt their own blockchain solutions, resulting in inefficiencies and complications in data sharing and collaboration.

Ensuring compatibility and coherence across multiple platforms is essential for realizing the full potential of blockchain in government.

Public perception and trust also play a critical role in the implementation of blockchain in government. Citizens may be skeptical about the security and privacy of their data on a blockchain system, especially in sensitive areas like voting and public records. Building trust requires not only robust security measures but also clear communication about how blockchain works and the benefits it offers. Governments must engage with the public to address concerns and demonstrate the advantages of adopting this technology, ensuring transparency throughout the implementation process.

Finally, the political landscape can significantly influence the adoption of blockchain in government. Different political agendas and priorities can create resistance to change, particularly in systems that are already functioning, albeit imperfectly. There may be concerns about the potential for job losses as blockchain automates processes traditionally handled by civil servants. Political will is crucial for overcoming these obstacles, and leaders must champion the use of blockchain, highlighting its potential to enhance efficiency, reduce corruption, and improve service delivery to citizens.

Chapter 9: Cybersecurity: Understanding Blockchain's Security Features Versus Potential Vulnerabilities

Blockchain Security Fundamentals

Blockchain technology has emerged as a transformative force across various sectors, but its security fundamentals remain a critical aspect for stakeholders. At its core, blockchain operates on a decentralized ledger system, which inherently enhances security by distributing data across multiple nodes instead of storing it in a single central repository. This decentralization mitigates the risks associated with single points of failure, making it considerably harder for malicious actors to alter or tamper with data. Each block in the chain is cryptographically linked to its predecessor, ensuring that any attempt at modification is immediately evident due to the invalidation of subsequent blocks. This feature plays a pivotal role in sectors such as financial services and supply chain management, where data integrity is paramount.

In the context of financial services, the implications of blockchain security are profound. The technology facilitates secure transactions, reducing the risk of fraud and enhancing trust between parties. Smart contracts, self-executing contracts with the terms of the agreement directly written into code, further bolster security by automating processes and reducing the need for intermediaries. However, investors must also be aware of potential vulnerabilities, such as coding errors in smart contracts or exploits in the underlying protocols. Understanding these risks is essential for developing robust investment strategies that leverage blockchain's advantages while mitigating its challenges.

Supply chain management significantly benefits from blockchain's security attributes, particularly in enhancing transparency and traceability. By utilizing blockchain, companies can create a tamper-proof record of every transaction, allowing stakeholders to track the provenance of goods from production to delivery. This transparency not only helps in preventing fraud but also in ensuring compliance with regulatory requirements. However, the implementation of blockchain in logistics is not without its challenges, including the necessity for collaboration among various stakeholders and the integration of existing systems. Investors and corporations must weigh these factors when considering blockchain solutions in their supply chain strategies.

In the healthcare sector, blockchain's promise for patient data security and interoperability presents another critical area of focus. Blockchain can safeguard sensitive patient information through encryption and access controls, ensuring that only authorized individuals can view or modify data. This level of security is vital in navigating the complexities of patient consent and data sharing across different healthcare providers. Nevertheless, concerns regarding the scalability of blockchain solutions and the potential for data breaches remain prevalent. Investors must remain vigilant in assessing the maturity of blockchain applications in healthcare and their ability to address these security concerns effectively.

Finally, the implications of blockchain extend to digital identity management, where security is paramount. Blockchain-based identity solutions offer enhanced protection against identity theft and fraud by providing users with greater control over their personal information. However, the transition to such systems raises questions about privacy and the potential misuse of data. As blockchain technology continues to evolve, understanding its security fundamentals will be crucial for stakeholders across sectors, including government initiatives, cybersecurity efforts, and emerging applications in energy trading and media rights management. Investors and organizations must stay informed about these developments to navigate the complex landscape of blockchain security effectively.

Common Vulnerabilities and Threats

Common vulnerabilities and threats within the blockchain landscape present significant considerations for various stakeholders, including investors, corporations, and educational institutions. One of the most prominent vulnerabilities is the risk of smart contract flaws. Smart contracts, which are self-executing contracts with the terms directly written into code, can contain bugs or coding errors that lead to unintended financial losses. Investors engaging in decentralized finance (DeFi) or other blockchain-based applications must remain vigilant about these vulnerabilities, as they can be exploited by malicious actors, resulting in the theft of funds or disruption of services.

Another critical threat arises from the potential for 51% attacks, particularly in proof-of-work blockchain systems. If a single entity or group gains control over the majority of the network's mining power, they can manipulate transactions, double-spend coins, and undermine the integrity of the blockchain. This risk is especially pertinent for smaller, less secure blockchains, where achieving a majority may be more feasible. Investors should consider the security measures and consensus mechanisms of the blockchains they are engaging with, as these factors can significantly influence the overall safety of their investments.

Phishing attacks also pose a substantial risk to blockchain users. Cybercriminals often employ social engineering tactics to trick individuals into revealing private keys or sensitive information, leading to the loss of assets. As the blockchain ecosystem grows, so does the sophistication of these attacks. Education on recognizing and avoiding phishing attempts is critical for all stakeholders, including investors, corporations, and educational institutions that may be integrating blockchain technology into their operations.

Furthermore, the intersection of blockchain and cybersecurity highlights both the protective features and vulnerabilities of the technology. While blockchain offers enhanced security through decentralization and cryptographic techniques, issues such as wallet security and human error remain prevalent. Investors must be aware of the importance of securing their private keys and utilizing reputable wallets, as failure to do so can result in irreversible losses. Additionally, organizations need to implement robust security practices to safeguard their blockchain implementations against potential breaches.

Finally, regulatory threats can affect the stability and viability of blockchain projects. As governments around the world grapple with how to regulate blockchain technologies, uncertainty can lead to market volatility and impact investment strategies. Stakeholders must stay informed about regulatory developments and assess how these changes could affect their respective sectors, from financial services to healthcare and beyond. Understanding these common vulnerabilities and threats is essential for navigating the blockchain landscape effectively and capitalizing on its potential benefits while mitigating risks.

Best Practices for Securing Blockchain Applications

Securing blockchain applications is paramount to ensuring the integrity and reliability of transactions across various sectors. Given the decentralized nature of blockchain technology, traditional security measures may not be sufficient. Investors, corporations, and IT professionals must adopt a multi-faceted approach to security that includes rigorous coding practices, comprehensive audits, and the implementation of robust cryptographic techniques. By prioritizing security from the outset, stakeholders can mitigate risks associated with vulnerabilities that may arise during the development and deployment of blockchain solutions.

One of the best practices for securing blockchain applications involves incorporating rigorous testing and auditing phases throughout the development lifecycle. Static and dynamic analysis tools can identify potential vulnerabilities in the code before they are exploited. Additionally, conducting regular security audits by third-party firms can provide an unbiased evaluation of the application's security posture. These audits should encompass both the smart contracts and the underlying blockchain infrastructure, ensuring that all components are scrutinized for weaknesses. Continuous monitoring post-deployment is equally vital, allowing teams to respond promptly to any emerging threats.

Encryption plays a crucial role in securing blockchain applications, particularly in sectors like healthcare and finance, where sensitive data is frequently handled. Utilizing advanced cryptographic methods such as public-private key pairs can protect user identities and transactions. Furthermore, implementing zero-knowledge proofs can enhance privacy by enabling parties to validate transactions without revealing any underlying data. This is especially pertinent in contexts such as digital identity verification and patient data management, where confidentiality is essential. Investors should be aware of how these encryption techniques can strengthen the security framework of blockchain applications.

Another essential practice is the establishment of clear access controls and permissions. Smart contracts should be designed with the principle of least privilege in mind, ensuring that users and applications are granted only the access necessary for their roles. This minimizes the risk of unauthorized transactions and data breaches. The use of multi-signature wallets can also add an additional layer of security, requiring multiple approvals for critical operations. In industries like real estate and supply chain management, where transaction integrity is vital, implementing these access control mechanisms can prevent fraudulent activities and bolster trust among stakeholders.

Finally, fostering a culture of security awareness is critical for the success of blockchain applications. Training and educating all participants involved in the blockchain ecosystem—including developers, investors, and end-users—on best practices for security can significantly reduce human error, which is often the weakest link in security protocols. Organizations should prioritize ongoing education and awareness initiatives, highlighting the latest threats and effective countermeasures. By building a knowledgeable community around blockchain applications, stakeholders can collectively enhance the security landscape and ensure the longevity and reliability of their investments in this innovative technology.

Chapter 10: Energy Sector: The Influence of Blockchain on Renewable Energy Trading and Distribution

Facilitating Decentralized Energy Trading

Facilitating decentralized energy trading through blockchain technology is poised to revolutionize the energy sector by enabling peer-to-peer transactions between consumers and producers. This shift allows individuals to buy and sell excess energy generated from renewable sources, such as solar panels, without the need for traditional intermediaries like utilities. By utilizing smart contracts on a blockchain platform, transactions can be executed automatically based on predefined conditions, ensuring transparency and efficiency while reducing costs. This decentralized approach not only democratizes energy access but also encourages investment in renewable technologies, further driving the transition toward sustainable energy systems.

Investors are increasingly recognizing the potential for decentralized energy trading to disrupt the current energy market structure. Traditional utility models often rely on centralized generation and distribution, which can lead to inefficiencies and higher costs for consumers. In contrast, blockchain-based platforms facilitate a more fluid market where energy can be traded in real-time, responding to supply and demand dynamics. This increased efficiency can lead to reduced energy prices, providing an attractive proposition for investors looking to capitalize on the growing demand for renewable energy solutions. Moreover, the ability to track and verify energy generation and consumption through blockchain enhances trust among participants, further promoting market participation.

Despite the promising prospects, several challenges must be addressed to fully realize the potential of decentralized energy trading. Regulatory frameworks vary significantly across regions, and many existing policies were not designed to accommodate peer-to-peer energy transactions. Investors and stakeholders must navigate a complex landscape of regulations that may hinder the rapid adoption of blockchain solutions in energy trading. Additionally, the scalability and interoperability of different blockchain platforms pose technical challenges that need to be overcome to ensure seamless transactions across various networks. Addressing these hurdles is essential for creating a robust ecosystem that fosters innovation and attracts investment in decentralized energy solutions.

Furthermore, the integration of blockchain technology into energy trading raises important considerations regarding cybersecurity. While blockchain is known for its security features, the decentralized nature of the technology also introduces new vulnerabilities, particularly if not implemented correctly. Investors and corporations must remain vigilant against potential threats that could compromise the integrity of energy transactions. Ensuring robust cybersecurity measures and adopting best practices in blockchain implementation will be crucial for maintaining trust among participants and safeguarding sensitive data related to energy trading.

In conclusion, facilitating decentralized energy trading through blockchain technology presents significant opportunities for investors and stakeholders across various sectors. The ability to enable peer-to-peer energy transactions not only supports the growth of renewable energy but also challenges traditional market structures, fostering a more competitive and efficient energy landscape. However, to harness these benefits fully, it is vital to address regulatory, technical, and security challenges. By doing so, investors can position themselves at the forefront of a transformative shift in the energy sector, aligning with broader trends toward sustainability and innovation in 2025 and beyond.

Enhancing Energy Distribution Efficiency

Enhancing energy distribution efficiency is a critical focus area as the world transitions towards sustainable energy solutions.

Blockchain technology presents a transformative opportunity in this sector by enabling decentralized energy trading platforms that allow consumers to buy and sell surplus energy directly. This peer-to-peer model not only democratizes energy distribution but also fosters competition, leading to lower prices and improved efficiency. By eliminating intermediaries, blockchain facilitates real-time transactions, reducing the latency often associated with traditional energy markets. Investors looking at the energy sector in 2025 must consider how these innovations can streamline operations and enhance profitability.

In addition to facilitating transactions, blockchain enhances transparency in energy distribution. Each transaction is recorded on a public ledger, which can be accessed by all participants in the network. This transparency helps to build trust among consumers and producers, as it provides verifiable data regarding energy sources and transactions. Such clarity is particularly important in the renewable energy space, where consumers increasingly prefer to source energy from sustainable providers. For corporations and investors, understanding the implications of this transparency can inform strategic decisions, especially as regulatory bodies and consumers demand more accountability in energy sourcing.

The integration of blockchain with smart grid technology further amplifies its potential to enhance energy distribution efficiency. Smart grids utilize real-time data to manage electricity demand and supply dynamically. When combined with blockchain, these systems can optimize energy flows, automatically adjusting to changes in usage patterns and integrating renewable energy sources more effectively. This synergy not only enhances operational efficiencies but also reduces the risk of outages and increases the resilience of energy systems. For stakeholders in the energy sector, investing in these technologies can lead to significant long-term benefits.

However, the implementation of blockchain in energy distribution is not without challenges. Issues such as scalability, regulatory hurdles, and the need for standardization must be addressed to fully realize its potential. Investors and corporations must navigate these complexities to develop viable blockchain solutions that meet both market demands and regulatory requirements. Collaboration among industry stakeholders, including technology providers, energy companies, and regulatory bodies, will be crucial in overcoming these barriers and ensuring a smooth transition to blockchain-enhanced energy systems.

Finally, as blockchain continues to evolve, its role in enhancing energy distribution efficiency will likely expand. Innovations such as tokenization of energy assets and the use of smart contracts for automatic settlements offer promising avenues for further efficiency gains. For investors, staying informed about these developments will be essential in identifying opportunities within the evolving energy landscape. As we progress toward 2025, the ability to leverage blockchain for improved energy distribution will not only enhance operational efficiencies but also contribute to broader sustainability goals, making it a critical area for investment and exploration.

Regulatory and Technical Challenges

Regulatory and technical challenges significantly influence the adoption and integration of blockchain technology across various sectors. As blockchain continues to gain traction in 2025, investors, corporations, and institutions must navigate a complex landscape marked by evolving regulations. Governments worldwide are grappling with how to categorize and regulate blockchain applications, leading to a patchwork of laws that can create uncertainty for businesses looking to innovate. This regulatory ambiguity can hinder investment strategies, as companies may be reluctant to allocate resources to projects that could be subject to sudden regulatory shifts. For investors, understanding these regulatory frameworks is essential for assessing the viability of blockchain ventures.

Technical challenges also pose significant barriers to widespread blockchain adoption. Scalability remains a critical issue, particularly for public blockchains that must process thousands of transactions per second. The infrastructure required to support such high transaction volumes is still under development. Additionally, interoperability between different blockchain platforms is a major hurdle that must be addressed. Without seamless integration, the potential for blockchain to revolutionize sectors like financial services, supply chain management, and healthcare is diminished. Investors must be aware of these technical limitations, as they directly impact the feasibility and timeline of blockchain implementations.

In the financial services sector, the impact of blockchain on banking and investment strategies is profound but fraught with regulatory complications. Financial institutions are exploring blockchain for its potential to enhance transaction efficiency and transparency. However, regulatory scrutiny over digital currencies and initial coin offerings can lead to cautious approaches from banks and investors alike. The interplay between innovation and regulation requires a nuanced understanding of how blockchain can be leveraged while conforming to legal standards. Investors must stay informed about regulatory developments to make educated decisions in this evolving market.

The healthcare industry faces unique regulatory and technical challenges related to patient data security and interoperability. Blockchain offers promising solutions for secure data sharing among healthcare providers, but compliance with health information privacy regulations, such as HIPAA in the United States, remains paramount. Technical issues such as data standardization and system integration must also be addressed to realize the full potential of blockchain in healthcare. Investors should consider these factors when evaluating healthcare blockchain projects, as successful implementations will require not only technological innovation but also legal adherence.

In the realm of digital identity, blockchain technology presents both advantages and risks. While blockchain can enhance the security and privacy of identity management systems, regulatory concerns regarding data ownership and consent can complicate its implementation. The lack of a unified regulatory framework for digital identities across jurisdictions may deter organizations from adopting blockchain-based solutions. Investors must weigh the potential benefits of improved identity verification against the regulatory landscape and technical challenges facing the sector. Understanding these complexities will be vital for making informed investment choices as blockchain continues to evolve.

Chapter 11: Digital Identity: The Advantages and Risks of Blockchain-Based Identity Solutions

Benefits of Decentralized Digital Identities

Decentralized digital identities present a transformative approach to identity management, offering numerous benefits across various sectors. One of the most significant advantages is enhanced privacy and control. Unlike traditional identity systems, where personal data is often stored in centralized databases vulnerable to breaches, decentralized identities allow individuals to own and manage their information. This self-sovereign identity model empowers users to share only the necessary data with service providers, reducing the risk of data abuse and enhancing user trust in digital interactions.

Another key benefit is improved security. Decentralized digital identities leverage blockchain's inherent security features, including cryptographic algorithms that ensure data integrity and authenticity. This reduces the likelihood of identity theft and fraud, which are prevalent in conventional identity systems. For investors and corporations, adopting such identities can lead to lower costs associated with data breaches and identity verification processes, ultimately fostering a more secure environment for transactions and interactions in sectors like finance, healthcare, and real estate.

Moreover, decentralized digital identities can facilitate streamlined processes across industries. In financial services, for instance, the ability to verify an individual's identity in real-time can expedite loan approvals and KYC (Know Your Customer) procedures, enhancing operational efficiency. In healthcare, secure and interoperable digital identities can revolutionize patient data management, allowing for seamless sharing of medical records among providers while maintaining strict privacy controls. Such efficiencies not only improve user experiences but can also lead to substantial cost savings for organizations.

The potential for inclusivity is another compelling advantage of decentralized digital identities. In many regions, individuals lack access to traditional identity systems, which can limit their participation in the digital economy. Blockchain-based identities can provide a solution by enabling individuals to create verifiable identities without relying on centralized authorities. This inclusiveness can foster greater economic participation and empower marginalized populations, aligning with the goals of many corporations and governments aiming to promote social equity.

Lastly, decentralized digital identities contribute to enhanced transparency and accountability. In sectors like government and supply chain management, blockchain's immutable ledger can provide a verifiable record of identity transactions, promoting trust among stakeholders. This transparency can significantly reduce fraudulent activities and enhance compliance with regulations. As organizations increasingly seek to build trust with customers and partners, the adoption of decentralized digital identities could serve as a crucial step in achieving these objectives while also paving the way for innovative solutions that leverage the full potential of blockchain technology.

Privacy Concerns and Data Management

Privacy concerns and data management have emerged as critical topics in the discourse surrounding blockchain technology, particularly as its applications expand across various sectors. With the increasing adoption of blockchain in financial services, supply chain management, healthcare, real estate, education, government, and more, understanding how data is stored and managed on decentralized networks is essential. Investors and corporations must grasp the implications of these privacy issues, as they can significantly affect investment strategies and operational frameworks. The immutable nature of blockchain, while fostering transparency, raises questions about the confidentiality of sensitive information and the potential for data breaches.

In the financial services sector, the integration of blockchain has transformed traditional banking and investment strategies. While blockchain can enhance transaction efficiency and reduce fraud, it also necessitates a reevaluation of privacy protocols. Investors must be aware that while transaction details on public blockchains are transparent, associated personal data may be exposed if not properly managed. This duality presents a challenge for financial institutions that must balance the benefits of increased transparency with the need to protect customer data from unauthorized access.

Supply chain management is another area where blockchain's promise of transparency poses privacy challenges. As companies track products from origin to destination, sensitive business information may inadvertently become accessible to competitors or malicious actors. Stakeholders need to establish robust data governance frameworks that allow for the necessary transparency in logistics while safeguarding proprietary information. This balancing act is crucial for maintaining competitive advantage and ensuring compliance with privacy regulations.

Healthcare represents a particularly sensitive domain where blockchain can enhance patient data security and interoperability. However, the sharing of health records on a blockchain raises significant privacy concerns. Investors in health tech must consider how blockchain solutions can offer secure data storage without compromising patient confidentiality. Solutions such as permissioned blockchains may mitigate some risks, but the complexities of healthcare regulations and patient rights necessitate careful planning and implementation to protect sensitive information.

As blockchain technology continues to evolve, the implications for digital identity and cybersecurity cannot be overlooked. Blockchain-based identity solutions offer a promising avenue for enhanced security and user control over personal information. Nevertheless, the potential for vulnerabilities, such as smart contract exploits or network attacks, remains a pertinent concern. Investors, tech industry professionals, and academic institutions must collaborate to develop best practices for data management that prioritize privacy while leveraging the benefits of blockchain technology across various sectors. Understanding these dynamics will be essential for navigating the blockchain landscape effectively in 2025 and beyond.

The Future of Digital Identity Solutions

The future of digital identity solutions is poised for transformation as blockchain technology continues to evolve and integrate into various sectors. With the growing demand for secure, verifiable, and user-centric identity systems, blockchain offers a decentralized approach that enhances privacy and control for individuals. As investors and industry professionals look to 2025, understanding the implications of blockchain-based digital identity solutions becomes crucial, especially considering the potential to reshape how identities are verified, managed, and utilized across multiple domains.

One of the primary advantages of blockchain in digital identity is its ability to provide a single, immutable record of identity that is easily accessible and verifiable. This is particularly beneficial in sectors such as healthcare and finance, where identity verification is critical for compliance and security. For instance, patients can have control over their medical records, granting access to healthcare providers while maintaining their privacy. Similarly, financial institutions can streamline customer onboarding processes, reducing fraud risks and improving customer experiences. This shift towards a blockchain-enabled identity framework can lead to significant cost savings and improved operational efficiencies for organizations.

However, the transition to blockchain-based digital identity systems is not without challenges. Issues such as scalability, interoperability, and regulatory compliance must be addressed to ensure widespread adoption. Moreover, while blockchain enhances security features, it is not immune to vulnerabilities, including potential attacks on the underlying infrastructure or the misuse of personal data. Investors and corporations must remain vigilant in assessing the risks associated with implementing these solutions, balancing the benefits of enhanced security against the possibility of new forms of cyber threats.

In the context of government applications, blockchain can revolutionize how public records, voter registrations, and identity verification are managed. By providing a transparent and tamper-proof system, governments can enhance trust and reduce instances of fraud. However, the integration of blockchain into public services raises concerns about data governance, privacy, and the digital divide. Stakeholders must carefully evaluate the implications of these systems to ensure equitable access and protection of citizens' rights.

As we look to the future, the role of digital identity solutions powered by blockchain will likely expand across industries, including education and entertainment. In education, blockchain can facilitate the verification of academic credentials, combating fraud and simplifying the hiring process for employers. In the entertainment sector, blockchain can redefine copyright management and content distribution, ensuring that creators are fairly compensated for their work. Overall, digital identity solutions hold great promise, but a nuanced understanding of their advantages and risks will be essential for stakeholders navigating this evolving landscape in 2025.

Chapter 12: Entertainment and Media: Effects of Blockchain on Copyright Management and Content Distribution

Revolutionizing Copyright Management

Revolutionizing copyright management through blockchain technology presents a transformative opportunity for the entertainment and media industries. Traditional copyright systems are often fraught with inefficiencies, lengthy processes, and obfuscation, leading to disputes over ownership and revenue distribution. By harnessing blockchain's decentralized ledger capabilities, stakeholders can establish a more transparent and immediate framework for tracking intellectual property rights. This transparency not only enhances trust among creators, producers, and consumers but also reduces the potential for disputes over copyright infringement, ultimately fostering a healthier ecosystem for artistic expression.

One of the key advantages of implementing blockchain in copyright management is the ability to create immutable records of ownership and usage. Each piece of content can be assigned a unique digital identifier on the blockchain, allowing for real-time tracking of how and when it is used. This capability not only simplifies the licensing process but also ensures that creators receive fair compensation for their work. Smart contracts can automate payment distribution based on predefined conditions, significantly reducing the administrative burden associated with traditional royalty collection processes. Thus, blockchain can streamline operations and ensure that artists are rewarded promptly and accurately.

However, integrating blockchain into existing copyright frameworks is not without challenges. The transition requires significant investment in technology and education for all stakeholders involved, from creators to distributors. Moreover, there is a need for industry-wide standards to ensure interoperability among different blockchain platforms. As various players in the entertainment and media sectors adopt diverse technological solutions, the risk of fragmentation increases, potentially undermining the very transparency that blockchain seeks to promote. Investors and corporations must therefore assess these challenges while strategizing their involvement in blockchain initiatives.

Moreover, the impact of blockchain on copyright management extends beyond financial implications. It fundamentally alters the relationship between creators and audiences, as consumers are given unprecedented access to the provenance of content. This shift can empower audiences to engage more meaningfully with the works they consume, creating a more informed community of supporters for artists. However, this increased transparency also raises concerns about privacy and the potential misuse of data. Stakeholders must navigate these ethical considerations carefully to maintain a balance between transparency and the protection of individual rights.

In conclusion, while blockchain technology holds immense promise for revolutionizing copyright management in the entertainment and media sectors, its adoption must be approached with caution. Investors, tech industry professionals, and educational institutions must collaboratively develop frameworks that address both the opportunities and challenges presented by blockchain. As the landscape evolves, ongoing dialogue and innovation will be essential to harness the full potential of blockchain, ensuring a fairer and more efficient copyright system that benefits all parties involved.

Enhancing Fair Compensation for Creators

Enhancing fair compensation for creators in the blockchain landscape is an essential consideration for stakeholders across various sectors. The traditional models of content creation and distribution often lead to discrepancies in how artists and creators are compensated for their work. With the advent of blockchain technology, there is an opportunity to create transparent systems that facilitate fair payment structures. Smart contracts can automate royalty payments, ensuring that creators receive timely compensation based on the terms laid out in their agreements. This shift not only enhances fairness but also builds trust between creators and consumers, fostering a more sustainable ecosystem in creative industries.

In the realm of entertainment and media, blockchain has the potential to revolutionize copyright management. By creating immutable records of ownership, blockchain can help combat piracy and unauthorized use of content. Each time a piece of content is utilized, smart contracts can trigger automatic payments to the original creator, ensuring they are fairly compensated for every instance of usage. This model not only encourages creators to produce more content but also incentivizes quality, as consumers are more likely to support creators who receive fair compensation for their work.

Moreover, the educational sector stands to benefit significantly from blockchain technology in credential verification. As institutions increasingly adopt blockchain to manage academic records, students can possess verifiable credentials that are tamper-proof and easily shareable with potential employers. This level of transparency can lead to a more equitable job market, where candidates are evaluated based on merit rather than potentially flawed or unverifiable qualifications. Consequently, educators can also receive fair compensation for their contributions to student success, as the system can track and reward effective teaching practices.

In supply chain management, transparency is crucial for establishing fair compensation among all parties involved in the production process. By utilizing blockchain, stakeholders can monitor the journey of a product from creation to sale, ensuring that each contributor in the supply chain is compensated fairly. This transparency helps to build accountability and trust among suppliers, manufacturers, and retailers, ultimately leading to more stable pricing models and a reduction in exploitation of workers at various levels of production.

Finally, the impact of blockchain on digital identity management can facilitate fair compensation models across multiple sectors. By allowing creators to maintain control over their digital identities and how their work is distributed, blockchain can empower individuals to negotiate better terms and receive fair compensation directly from consumers. This direct relationship not only enhances the creator's earning potential but also enriches the consumer experience, as buyers are more likely to support creators whose work they value and trust. As blockchain continues to evolve, the focus on enhancing fair compensation for creators will remain a cornerstone in building equitable systems across diverse industries.

Challenges in Adoption by Media Industries

The integration of blockchain technology within the media industries presents a range of challenges that can impede its widespread adoption. One of the primary issues is the existing infrastructure of traditional media organizations, which often relies on established practices that may not align with the decentralized nature of blockchain. Transitioning from legacy systems to a blockchain-based framework requires substantial investment in new technologies and training, which can deter companies from making the leap. Furthermore, the reluctance to disrupt existing workflows can stifle innovation, leaving media organizations at risk of falling behind competitors who embrace digital transformations more readily.

Another significant challenge is the regulatory landscape surrounding blockchain technology. Media industries are subject to numerous laws and regulations that govern content distribution, copyright, and data privacy. The introduction of blockchain raises complex legal questions regarding ownership rights, intellectual property, and compliance with varying jurisdictional laws. Investors and corporations must navigate these uncertainties to ensure that blockchain implementations do not inadvertently contravene existing regulations, which can lead to costly legal battles and reputational damage.

The issue of scalability also poses a hurdle for blockchain adoption in the media sector. While blockchain offers promising solutions for content distribution and copyright management, the technology is still evolving. Many blockchain platforms face limitations in processing speed and transaction volume, which can hinder their ability to support large-scale media operations. As audiences demand real-time access to content, the inability of blockchain systems to handle high traffic can lead to frustration and diminished user experience, ultimately affecting the bottom line for media companies.

Interoperability between different blockchain networks is another challenge that media industries must confront. Various platforms may offer unique features and benefits, but the lack of standardized protocols can complicate collaboration and data sharing. This fragmentation can create silos, preventing media companies from fully capitalizing on blockchain's potential to enhance transparency and efficiency in content management. Investors and stakeholders must recognize this challenge and advocate for industry-wide standards to facilitate smoother integration and interoperability across platforms.

Lastly, public perception and understanding of blockchain technology present a barrier to its adoption in the media sphere. Many stakeholders, including consumers and industry professionals, may have limited knowledge of how blockchain operates and its benefits. Misinformation and skepticism can lead to resistance against adopting new technologies, which hampers progress. Educational initiatives and transparent communication about blockchain's advantages, particularly in protecting intellectual property and ensuring fair compensation for creators, are essential for fostering a more informed environment that encourages adoption and innovation in the media industries.

Chapter 13: Conclusion: The Future of Blockchain for Investors in 2025

Key Takeaways for Investors

Investors in 2025 must recognize the multifaceted nature of blockchain technology and its implications across various sectors. Understanding the pros and cons of blockchain is essential for making informed investment decisions. As the technology matures, its potential to disrupt traditional industries becomes clearer. Investors should focus on sectors such as financial services, where blockchain is revolutionizing banking and investment strategies, offering new avenues for efficiency and transparency. The ability to streamline transactions and reduce costs can significantly impact profit margins and operational effectiveness.

In supply chain management, blockchain's promise of enhanced transparency and traceability presents both opportunities and challenges. By allowing real-time tracking of goods and verification of authenticity, blockchain can reduce fraud and improve accountability. However, investors must be cautious of the implementation hurdles and resistance from established players in the logistics industry. Understanding these dynamics is crucial for assessing the viability and potential return on investment in blockchain-based supply chain solutions.

Healthcare is another sector where blockchain offers transformative potential, particularly in enhancing patient data security and interoperability among various systems. The decentralization of health records can empower patients while ensuring privacy and compliance with regulations. Investors should evaluate companies that are developing blockchain solutions for healthcare, considering their ability to navigate regulatory landscapes and the competitive advantages they may hold in this evolving market.

In real estate, blockchain is changing how property transactions and ownership verification are conducted. By enabling digital deeds and smart contracts, blockchain can streamline the buying and selling process, reduce fraud, and lower transaction costs. However, the transition from traditional practices to blockchain-based solutions may face legal and regulatory challenges. Investors should analyze the readiness of the real estate market to adopt these innovations and the potential impact on property values and investment strategies.

Lastly, the implications of blockchain extend to digital identity, entertainment, and public governance. Blockchain-based identity solutions can enhance security and privacy but also raise concerns about misuse and data integrity. In the entertainment sector, blockchain is reshaping copyright management and content distribution, presenting both opportunities and risks. For government applications, the potential for blockchain to improve public records and voting systems is significant, yet it requires careful consideration of security and accessibility. As these various sectors evolve, investors should remain vigilant and informed about the developments in blockchain technology to capitalize on its potential while mitigating risks.

The Role of Blockchain in Shaping Future Markets

The integration of blockchain technology is poised to revolutionize various markets, presenting both opportunities and challenges for investors and stakeholders across diverse sectors. In 2025, the ongoing maturation of blockchain systems will redefine how transactions are conducted, information is shared, and trust is established. Investors must grasp the implications of these changes to navigate future markets effectively. The decentralized nature of blockchain enhances transparency and security, making it particularly appealing in sectors such as financial services, supply chain management, and healthcare.

In financial services, blockchain's impact on banking and investment strategies cannot be overstated. The technology facilitates quicker transactions, reduces fees, and minimizes the risk of fraud. By enabling peer-to-peer transactions without intermediaries, blockchain has the potential to democratize access to financial services. Furthermore, smart contracts can automate complex financial arrangements, reducing the reliance on traditional legal frameworks. However, investors must remain vigilant about regulatory developments, which could either enhance or hinder blockchain's adoption in finance.

Supply chain management is another area where blockchain can significantly improve operational efficiency. By providing a transparent and immutable record of transactions, blockchain enhances traceability, allowing companies to verify the authenticity of products and streamline logistics. This increased transparency can lead to reduced fraud and improved compliance with regulatory standards. However, the challenge lies in the integration of blockchain with existing systems and the need for industry-wide collaboration to realize its full potential.

In the healthcare sector, blockchain holds promise for securing patient data and improving interoperability among systems. By enabling patients to control access to their medical records, blockchain can enhance privacy while ensuring that healthcare providers have the necessary information to deliver effective care. Despite these advantages, the industry faces hurdles, such as the need for standardization and the risk of data breaches inherent in any digital system. Investors should consider these factors when evaluating opportunities in healthcare-related blockchain projects.

The applications of blockchain extend to real estate, education, government, cybersecurity, the energy sector, digital identity, and entertainment. In real estate, blockchain simplifies property transactions and ownership verification, potentially reducing fraud and expediting processes. In education, it offers a reliable method for credential verification, enhancing the integrity of academic records. Governments are exploring blockchain for public records and voting systems, while the energy sector is leveraging it for renewable energy trading. However, each of these applications comes with its own set of challenges, including regulatory compliance and the need for robust cybersecurity measures. Understanding these dynamics is crucial for investors aiming to seize the opportunities presented by blockchain technology in future markets.

Final Thoughts on Navigating the Blockchain Landscape

As we conclude our exploration of the blockchain landscape in 2025, it is essential to reflect on the multifaceted implications this technology holds for various sectors. Investors, students, and corporations alike must recognize that while blockchain offers numerous advantages, it also presents significant challenges. Understanding these dynamics is critical for making informed decisions in an evolving market. The potential for innovation in financial services, supply chain management, healthcare, and beyond underscores the need for a well-rounded comprehension of blockchain's capabilities and limitations.

In the financial services sector, blockchain has the potential to transform banking and investment strategies by enhancing transaction speed and reducing costs. However, investors should remain cautious, as the volatility and regulatory uncertainties surrounding cryptocurrencies can pose risks. A comprehensive grasp of blockchain's impact on market structures and transaction methodologies can empower investors to navigate this complex landscape more effectively. As the technology matures, it is vital to stay informed about the developments that could influence investment opportunities and financial stability.

Supply chain management exemplifies another area where blockchain's promise of transparency can revolutionize logistics. By enabling real-time tracking and validation of goods, companies can enhance accountability and reduce fraud. Nevertheless, the implementation of blockchain solutions can be challenging, particularly concerning interoperability with existing systems and the need for industry-wide standards. Stakeholders must weigh the benefits of improved transparency against the potential hurdles of integrating new technologies into established processes, ensuring that any transition is both strategic and practical.

In healthcare, blockchain's implications for patient data security and interoperability are profound. The ability to securely store and share patient records can lead to improved care coordination and reduced administrative burdens. However, stakeholders must consider the ethical implications of data privacy and consent. As the healthcare industry increasingly leans on technology, a thorough understanding of blockchain's role in safeguarding sensitive information is paramount. This understanding will help ensure that the benefits of enhanced security do not come at the cost of patient trust and confidentiality.

Lastly, the influence of blockchain extends into various sectors such as real estate, education, government, cybersecurity, energy, digital identity, and entertainment. Each sector faces unique challenges and opportunities related to blockchain adoption. Investors and industry professionals must actively engage in ongoing education and dialogue to navigate these complexities. By fostering a culture of informed decision-making, stakeholders can better position themselves to leverage the benefits of blockchain while mitigating its risks, ensuring a balanced approach to embracing this transformative technology in 2025 and beyond.

www.ingramcontent.com/pod-product-compliance
Lightning Source LLC
Chambersburg PA
CBHW070409230526
45471CB00006B/2727